This book belongs to...

_____

ALONG For the RIDE

Written by Robert A. Vajgrt

Illustrated by Alyssa Brown

Along for the Ride

Published by Larger Than Life, LLC
Greenfield, Wisconsin, U.S.A.

VAJGRT, ROBERT A., Author
ALONG FOR THE RIDE
ROBERT A. VAJGRT

Larger Than Life, LLC
5212 South 41st Street
Greenfield, Wisconsin 53221
www.LargerThanLifeLLC.com

Library of Congress Control Number: 2025904857
ISBN: 979-8-9915549-8-5 (paperback)
ISBN: 979-8-9915549-9-2 (hardcover)
ISBN: 979-8-9915549-7-8 (digital)

JUVENILE NONFICTION / Family / Parents
JUVENILE NONFICTION / Inspirational & Personal Growth
JUVENILE NONFICTION / Social Topics / Values & Virtues

Illustrations and Book Design by Alyssa K Brown (creationsalyssas@gmail.com)
Edited by Lisa Shrewsberry (shrewsberry5live@gmail.com)
Publishing Management: Susie Schaefer (FinishTheBookPublishing.com)

QUANTITY PURCHASES: Schools, companies, professional groups, clubs, and other organizations may qualify for special terms when ordering quantities of this title. For information, email info@largerthanlifellc.com

To Bradley and Kaytlyn and those
who came along for the ride.
-Robert

To my Dad. You are one of my
favorite people.
-Alyssa

It feels like yesterday. It is the first of many rides to come. I tenderly buckle you in your car seat for your first day of daycare. You are quiet, only eight weeks old, my precious cargo.

As I hand you over cautiously and reluctantly to others who will guard and nurture you, it takes some doing. After all, you ARE precious cargo. And as I say goodbye, I try hard not to cry.

Oh the rides we share together! The sights we see, and the sounds you make. From sounds like phhaaaat, to words like momm-eee, to complete sentences.

Before we know it, four years of rides pass, and it's your sister's turn to join us on her way to daycare, only she isn't so quiet. She makes even more sounds than you! Now, she's along for the ride, too.

Now, it's your first day of Kindergarten! But another first must happen before we leave home —a photo on the front porch, one of many to come. We put on our brave faces and yours is even braver than mine.

We load up in the car, we three with the smell of crayons and freshly sharpened pencils.

I can't see, in my rearview mirror, how you are feeling inside, but I try hard not to cry.

Each day, it's just us, along with my briefcase, and your backpack, but no cargo as precious as your sister and you.

You don't know it yet, or maybe you do, but I'm just as excited and anxious as you for every "first" day that is to come...

Years go by of briefcases, backpacks, more firsts, and new passengers. We add classmates, friends, girlfriends, boyfriends and special guests like Johnny Cash (he's an acquired taste)... They, too, are all along for the ride.

On our rides are laughing, singing, joking, snacking, and sometimes the beauty of silence. We love one another, we learn from one another, and the comfort of our shared presence is the anchor before the storm of each busy day.

...and the cargo changes like seasons, treasure to be found sliding and hiding, clinking and clanking beneath the seats.

There are snacks, winter boots, uniforms, and backpacks...

But, sometimes, images in a mirror are the opposite of what they appear to be. Like how it appears to me now that all along, you were teaching me...

Soon, our cargo lightens—you become drivers with your own passengers, friends, and their stuff. Our rides are sometimes separate now as both of you explore and grow.

The time comes for an important stop along our ride.

It's the last day of school for you, my baby boy. Then, on another day, not too long after, it's the last day of school for you, my baby girl.

While driving away, I think it was not my son and daughter and their friends who were along for the ride— it was me.

...all the things you showed me...

All the places you took me...

....and yes, all the things you taught me. I would never have experienced all these things if it weren't for you.

... the days, glad and sad, the hearty laughs and the heartbreaks, the accomplishments and disappointments, the friends and advice... they're all still along for the ride. They are now my constant precious cargo, but still none as precious as you.

As I unbuckle the memories of passengers past, I realize what a ride it has been…

First Day!

Sad she can't join her brother.

Goal!

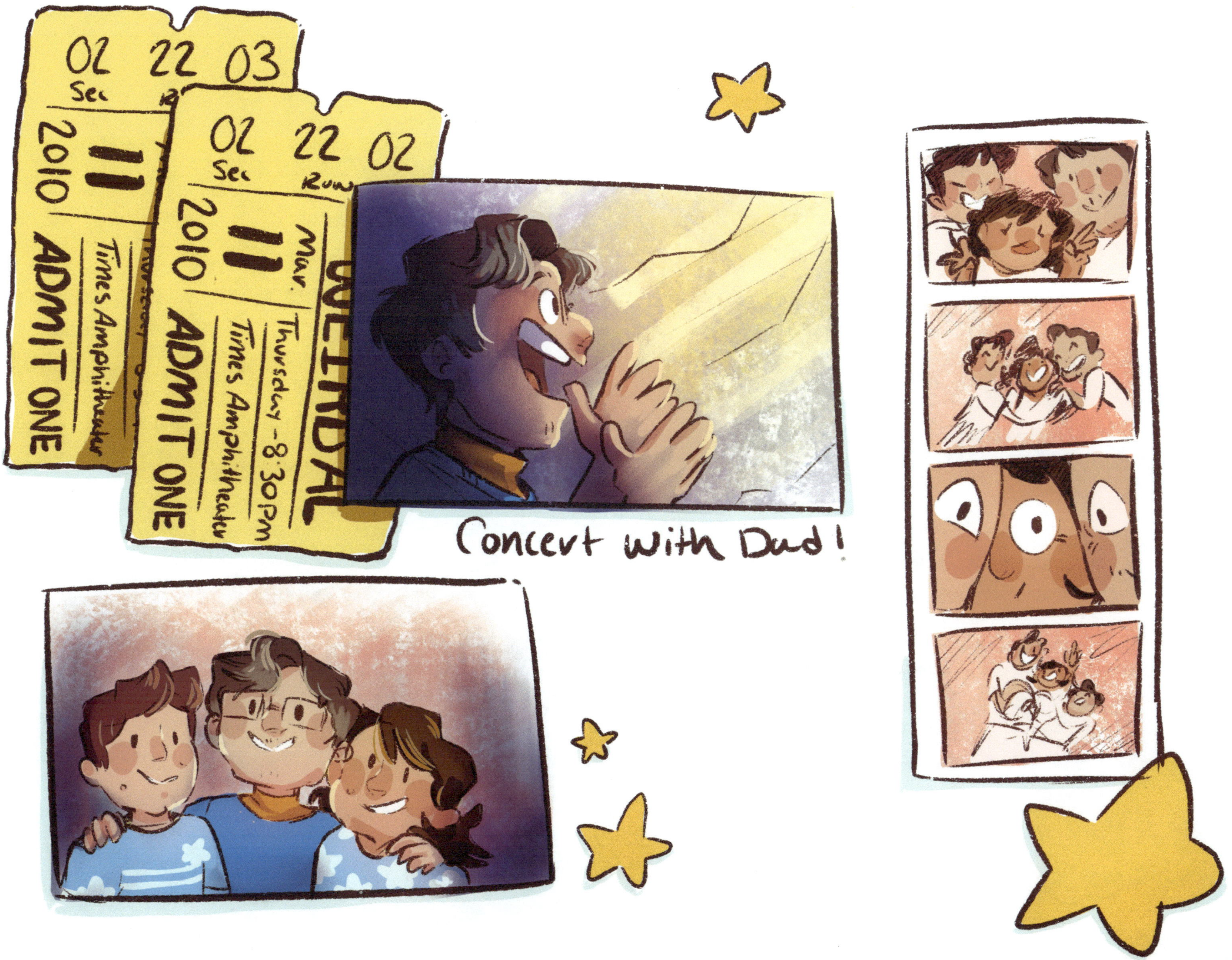

Concert with Dad!

Her last day!! ♥

I will miss you on my ride tomorrow, and I am forever
grateful for you allowing me to tag along for the
ride.